Yeats

Romantic Visionary

W. B. YEATS

First published in Great Britain by Brockhampton Press,
20 Bloomsbury Street, London WC1B 3QA.

Copyright © 1996 Brockhampton Press

This 1999 edition is published by Gramercy Books™, an imprint of
Random House Value Publishing, Inc., 201 East 50th Street, New York, N.Y. 10022.
Reprint 2000
Gramercy Books™ and colophon are trademarks of
Random House Value Publishing, Inc.

Random House
New York • Toronto • London • Sydney • Auckland
http://www.randomhouse.com/

Created and produced by Flame Tree Publishing,
part of The Foundry Creative Media Company Limited,
Crabtree Hall, Crabtree Lane, Fulham, London SW6 6TY.

Special thanks to
Kate Brown and Kelley Doak for their work on this series.

Printed and bound in U. A. E.

A CIP catalog record for this book is available from the Library of Congress.

ISBN 0-517-16110-9

8 7 6 5 4 3 2 1

Yeats
Romantic Visionary

Written and Compiled by
O. B. DUANE

Gramercy Books
New York

Contents

INTRODUCTION 6
AUTHOR'S NOTE 11
CHRONOLOGY 12

CROSSWAYS (1889)
Ephemera 14
The Stolen Child 16
Down by the Salley Gardens 19

THE ROSE (1893)
A Faery Song 20
Fergus and the Druid 22
Who Goes with Fergus 24
The Two Trees 26
The White Birds 28
The Countess Cathleen in Paradise 30
When You Are Old 32

THE WIND AMONG THE REEDS (1899)
The Cap and Bells 33
He Wishes for the Cloths of Heaven 35
The Lover Tells of the Rose in his Heart 36
The Fiddler of Dooney 38
The Song of Wandering Aengus 40

IN THE SEVEN WOODS (1904)
Never Give All the Heart 42
The Ragged Wood 44
O Do Not Love Too Long 44

THE GREEN HELMET AND OTHER POEMS (1910)
At Galway Races 45
No Second Troy 46
Words 47
A Woman Homer Sung 48

RESPONSIBILITIES (1914)
I To a Child Dancing in the Wind 50
II Two Years Later 50
The Cold Heaven 51
The Magi...51
The Mountain Tomb...52
On Those That Hated 'The Playboy of the Western World', 1907 53
September 1913 54
A Coat 56

THE WILD SWANS AT COOLE (1919)
The Wild Swans at Coole 58
An Irish Airman Foresees His Death 59
The Dawn 60
Broken Dreams 62

MICHAEL ROBARTES AND THE DANCER (1921)
Easter 1916..65
Under Saturn..68
A Prayer for My Daughter 69

THE TOWER (1928)
Sailing to Byzantium...73
Leda and the Swan 74
A Man Young and Old 75
Wisdom 80

THE WINDING STAIR (1933)
A Dialogue of Self and Soul...82
Death 85
Coole Park, 1929 86
The Crazed Moon 87

LAST POEMS (1936-9)
The Circus Animals' Desertion 88
Come Gather Round Me, Parnellites 91
Why Should Not Old Men Be Mad 92

INDEX TO FIRST LINES...94
NOTES ON ILLUSTRATIONS 96

Introduction

WILLIAM BUTLER YEATS was born in Sandymount, Dublin, the eldest of six children, only four of whom survived beyond infancy. His father, John Butler Yeats, came from a large Anglo-Protestant family in Co. Down. His mother, Susan Pollexfen, was the daughter of a well-to-do shipping merchant in Co. Sligo. When William was two years old, his father made the decision to abandon his career as a barrister and moved his family to London, where he hoped to establish a reputation for himself as a serious artist. For the next fourteen years until 1881, the Yeats household lived under continuous financial strain as John Butler Yeats struggled to support an expanding family on a few meagre commissions. During these difficult times, the children spent prolonged summer holidays with their mother's family in the west of Ireland. It was here that William Butler Yeats discovered traditions and a way of life he saw as preferable to his English upbringing. He allowed these influences to feed his poetic imagination intending one day to create a literature worthy of a country and a people he steadily grew to love.

William attended the Godolphin school in Hammersmith between the ages of twelve and fourteen. His father then decided to move back to Dublin and settled his family at Howth. He enrolled his eldest son at the Erasmus Smith High School and rented a small painter's studio for himself in York Street. The two travelled into Dublin city each morning, stopping for breakfast at the studio, where John Butler Yeats read aloud to William from the works of Shakespeare, Balzac and Blake. Although an inadequate provider for his family, he was a well-educated man, a witty conversationalist and he questioned established values. He

was unconcerned about money and encouraged his son to become a poet in spite of the inevitable financial insecurity.

Yeats began to write his first verses in his late teens. At about the same time he attended the Metropolitan School of Art. It was here that he met the visionary and poet George Russell (AE) with whom he formed a firm friendship fed by a mutual interest in the occult. He read A. P. Sinnett's *Esoteric Buddhism* which had a profound effect on him and began to attend meetings of the Dublin Hermetic Society. His father also introduced him to several of his old friends, including Edward Dowden, Professor of English Literature at Trinity College. Before long, Yeats was a regular contributor to the Contemporary Club, an intellectual circle of writers, poets and fledgling politicians who met weekly to discuss political, literary and philosophical matters. Yeats gave several poetry readings at these events and a number of his poems were published in the *Dublin University Review*.

Through the Contemporary Club, he was introduced to the Fenian activist, John O' Leary, one of the first men to acknowledge his poetic genius and certainly the first to encourage him to make liberal use of Irish themes. The young poet began to study Irish history and old Gaelic legends with enthusiasm. He concluded that literature and nationality were intertwined and began to write his own kind of verse, dreamy and idealistic to begin with, yet moving towards a deeper awareness of Ireland's spiritual and literary heritage.

In the spring of 1887, the family moved to London for a second time. Yeats was instantly attracted to William Morris's circle and met the leading figures of the Socialist movement, John Burns, the trades unionist, and George Bernard Shaw. He also became acquainted with other writers and editors, including Oscar Wilde, Lionel Johnson, Florence Farr and Edwin Ellis, with whom he edited Blake's poems. He frequented the house of Madame Blavatsky and joined her

Theosophical Lodge, an association set up to carry out experiments in occult practices.

His sense of Irishness intensified during his time in London, particularly after his meeting with Maud Gonne in January 1889. This beautiful, determined young woman was keen to meet the poet whose Gaelic legend, *The Wanderings of Oisin*, had just been published. At twenty-three, Maud Gonne was already deeply committed to Irish nationalism and was a formidable campaigner for social justice. Yeats fell passionately in love with her and came to view her as a symbol of Ireland. Their nationalist ideals fused in their belief that Ireland's identity could be revived, but their methods differed: Maud Gonne favoured a violent path, while Yeats sought to recreate a national literature that would draw together the shattered soul of the nation. Ultimately, however, he found himself becoming more and more involved in Ireland's political struggle under Maud Gonne's influence.

Several poems from *The Rose* were addressed to Maud Gonne who had refused Yeats' offer of marriage in 1891. A powerful sense of the poet's wounded pride pervades the verses, but the rose is also used as a symbol of Ireland and of intellectual beauty. Yeats, at this time, had also become heavily involved in the Irish Literary Society in London and Dublin and had joined the Irish Republican Brotherhood. He made numerous contributions to journals and newspapers in support of the writings of Irish authors. He founded the Rhymers' Club in London where he socialized with England's contemporary poets and was admitted to the Order of the Golden Dawn, a society dedicated to the study of ritual magic.

Yeats' poems towards the end of the 1890s had developed significantly in style and technique from his earlier, popular poetry. His varied interests in spiritualism, mysticism and mythology were now combined to produce more impenetrable and enigmatic works. The love poems to Maud

Gonne from *The Wind Among the Reeds* (1899) have a far more distilled quality. 'He Wishes for the Cloths of Heaven' is a beautifully sculpted, richly imagined expression of a calmer devotion that is not entirely without hope. By the time *In the Seven Woods* was published, however, Yeats' mood was again defeatist. He had become disillusioned with Irish politics, partly as a result of Maud Gonne's marriage to John MacBride in 1903, which hurt him deeply. He abandoned the lyrical language of his 'Celtic Twilight' in favour of a bleaker, more rhetorical style, emphasizing his love for Maud Gonne as a thing of the past.

In 1896, Yeats met Lady Gregory and became a regular visitor to her home at Coole Park. They collaborated to form an Irish National Theatre which resulted in the opening of the Abbey Theatre in 1907. Between 1904 and 1910 Yeats devoted much of his time to theatre business. He vigorously defended J. M. Synge when riots broke out at the performance of *The Playboy of the Western World* and fought a continuous battle with the authorities at Dublin Castle for freedom of artistic speech.

The disillusionment Yeats felt as he entered middle age was reflected in the volume of poems, *Responsibilities* (1914). He began to record the realities of Ireland, that 'blind, bitter land', in language stripped of subtlety and ornamentation. His unrequited love for Maud Gonne was always an underlying frustration and it was compounded when, in 1916, following her husband's execution after the Dublin Easter Rising, she once again refused to marry him.

The poet eventually married Georgie Hyde-Lees in 1917, a woman who shared his interest in mysticism and spiritualism. The union brought him fresh confidence and his poetry began to flourish anew. By the time he came to write 'Easter 1916' and 'A Prayer for My Daughter', his verses were a masterful blend of realism and intense personal emotion. The beauty of his earlier work now merged with an intellectual control to create a mature style of technical brilliance.

Yeats was appointed to the Senate in 1922 and was awarded the Nobel Prize for Literature in 1923. In his two later collections of poems, *The Tower* (1928) and *The Winding Stair* (1933) he wrote candidly of political change and disillusionment, of the vagaries of human passion, of old friends and distant memories, of the loss of youth and his increasing awareness of the coming of death. Even in his last years he remained supremely creative. Several of his later poems, often filled with self-mockery and devastating honesty, attempt to analyse his own life and to confront death with dignity. His self-written epitaph urges the horseman to remain heroic and to 'Cast a cold eye/On life, on death' – the cold eye of wisdom and detachment, not the warm, misty eye of sorrow and despair. At the time of his death in 1939, his standing as the greatest modern poet in the English language, and the greatest poet Ireland had ever produced, was undisputed.

Author's Note

From his earliest verses, to his last poems, Yeats' work immeasurably enriched Ireland's literary tradition and English literature as a whole. The poems chosen for this book, arranged in the order of Yeats' published collections, are representative of his major themes and concerns, and trace the evolution of his talent over the course of a career that spanned half a century.

Chronology

1865 William Butler Yeats born, 13 June in Sandymount, Dublin.

1884 Yeats attends the Metropolitan School of Art, Dublin.

1886 Yeats leaves the Metropolitan School of Art. *Mosada* is published in Dublin.

1887 Family moves to England. Yeats' first poem to be published in England, *The Madness of King Goll*, appears in 'The Leisure Hour'.

1889 *The Wanderings of Oisin and Other Poems* is published.

1891 Yeats founds the Irish Literary Society in London.

1892 Yeats founds the Irish Literary Society in Dublin. *The Countess Cathleen and Various Legends and Lyrics* are published.

1899 First production of the Irish Literary Theatre, *The Countess Cathleen*, is performed at the Ancient Concert

Rooms. *The Wind among the Reeds* is published.

1902   *Cathleen ni Houlihan* and *Deirdre* performed in Dublin. The Irish National Theatre becomes the Irish Literary Theatre with Yeats as president.

1903   *In the Seven Woods* (poems), *Baile and Aillinn* (narrative poem) and *Ideas of Good and Evil* (essays) are published.

1906   Yeats' *Poems 1899-1905* published. *The Shadowy Waters* (revised version) published.

1908   *Collected Works* published. Travels to Paris to work on *The Player Queen*.

1910   *The Green Helmet and Other Poems* is published.

1914   *Responsibilities* is published. Yeats begins his memoirs.

1917   Yeats marries Georgie Hyde-Lees in London in October.

1918   *Per Amica Silentia Lunae* published.

1919   Daughter, Anne, born in February. Yeats moves to Galway. *The Wild Swans at Coole* published.

1921   A son, Michael, born in August. Irish Free State established on 6 December. *Michael Robartes and the Dancer* is published.

1922   Outbreak of the Irish Civil War. Yeats family moves to Dublin. Yeats becomes a senator.

1923   Civil War ends. Yeats is awarded the Nobel Prize for Literature.

1925   *A Vision* is published.

1929   *A Packet for Ezra Pound* is published. *Fighting the Waves* is produced at the Abbey Theatre.

1933   *The Winding Stair and Other Poems* is published.

1935   *A Full Moon in March* is published.

1938   Yeats makes his last public appearance and leaves for the South of France in late November.

1939   Yeats dies on 28 January and is buried at Roquebrune in France.

1948   Yeats' body is brought to Ireland and re-interred at Drumcliffe Churchyard, Co. Sligo.

Ephemera

'YOUR eyes that once were never weary of mine
Are bowed in sorrow under pendulous lids,
Because our love is waning.'
And then she:
'Although our love is waning, let us stand
By the lone border of the lake once more,
Together in that hour of gentleness
When the poor tired child, Passion, falls asleep.
How far away the stars seem, and how far
Is our first kiss, and ah, how old my heart!'

Pensive they paced along the faded leaves,
While slowly he whose hand held hers replied:
'Passion has often worn our wandering hearts.'

The woods were round them, and the yellow leaves
Fell like faint meteors in the gloom, and once
A rabbit old and lame limped down the path;
Autumn was over him: and now they stood
On the lone border of the lake once more:
Turning, he saw that she had thrust dead leaves
Gathered in silence, dewy as her eyes,
In bosom and hair.
'Ah, do not mourn,' he said,
'That we are tired, for other loves await us;
Hate on and love through unrepining hours.
Before us lies eternity; our souls
Are love, and a continual farewell.'

The Stolen Child

WHERE dips the rocky highland
Of Sleuth Wood in the lake,
There lies a leafy island
Where flapping herons wake
The drowsy water-rats;
There we've hid our faery vats,
Full of berries
And of reddest stolen cherries.
Come away, O human child!
To the waters and the wild
With a faery, hand in hand,
For the world's more full of weeping than you
can understand.

Where the wave of moonlight glosses
The dim grey sands with light,
Far off by furthest Rosses
We foot it all the night,
Weaving olden dances,
Mingling hands and mingling glances
Till the moon has taken flight;
To and fro we leap
And chase the frothy bubbles,
While the world is full of troubles
And is anxious in its sleep.
Come away, O human child!
To the waters and the wild
With a faery, hand in hand,
For the world's more full of weeping than you
can understand.

Where the wandering water gushes
From the hills above Glen-Car,
In pools among the rushes
That scarce could bathe a star,
We seek for slumbering trout
And whispering in their ears
Give them unquiet dreams;
Leaning softly out
From ferns that drop their tears
Over the young streams.
Come away, O human child!
To the waters and the wild
With a faery, hand in hand,
For the world's more full of weeping than you
can understand.

Away with us he's going,
The solemn-eyed:
He'll hear no more the lowing
Of the calves on the warm hillside
Or the kettle on the hob
Sing peace into his breast,
Or see the brown mice bob
Round and round the oatmeal-chest.
For he comes, the human child,
To the waters and the wild
With a faery, hand in hand,
From a world more full of weeping than he
can understand.

Down By The Salley Gardens

Down by the salley gardens my love and I did meet;
She passed the salley gardens with little snow-white feet.
She bid me take love easy, as the leaves grow on the tree;
But I, being young and foolish, with her would not agree.

In a field by the river my love and I did stand,
And on my leaning shoulder she laid her snow-white hand.
She bid me take life easy, as the grass grows on the weirs;
But I was young and foolish, and now am full of tears.

A Faery Song

Sung by the people of Faery over Diarmuid and Grania,
in their bridal sleep under a Cromlech.

WE who are old, old and gay,
O so old!
Thousands of years, thousands of years,
If all were told:

Give to these children, new from the world,
Silence and love;

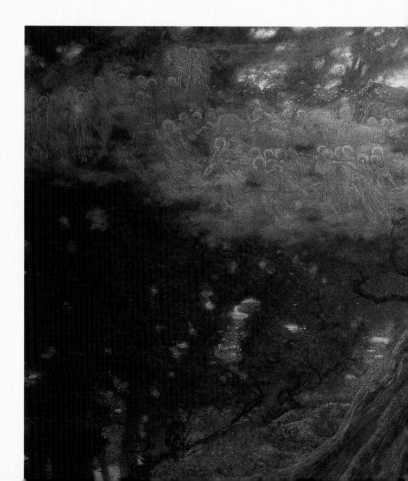

And the long dew-dropping hours of the night,
And the stars above:

Give to these children, new from the world,
Rest far from men.
Is anything better, anything better?
Tell us it then:

Us who are old, old and gay,
O so old!
Thousands of years, thousands of years,
If all were told.

Fergus and the Druid

Fergus. This whole day have I followed in the rocks,
And you have changed and flowed from shape to shape
First as a raven on whole ancient wings
Scarcely a feather lingered, then you seemed
A weasel moving on from stone to stone,
And now at last you wear a human shape,
A thin grey man half lost in gathering night.

Druid. What would you, king of the proud Red Branch kings?

Fergus. This would I say, most wise of living souls:
Young subtle Conchubar sat close by me
When I gave judgment, and his words were wise,
And what to me was burden without end,
To him seemed easy, so I laid the crown
Upon his head to cast away my sorrow.

Druid. What would you, king of the proud Red Branch kings?

Fergus. A king and proud! and that is my despair.
I feast amid my people on the hill,
And pace the woods, and drive my chariot-wheels
In the white border of the murmuring sea;
And still I feel the crown upon my head.

Druid. What would you, Fergus?

Fergus. Be no more a king
But learn the dreaming wisdom that is yours.

Druid. Look on my thin grey hair and hollow cheeks
   And on these hands that may not lift the sword,
     This body trembling like a wind-blown reed.
   No woman's loved me, no man sought my help.

     Fergus. A king is but a foolish labourer
   Who wastes his blood to be another's dream.

   Druid. Take, if you must, this little bag of dreams;
  Unloose the cord, and they will wrap you round.

    Fergus. I see my life go drifting like a river
From change to change; I have been many things—
   A green drop in the surge, a gleam of light
     Upon a sword, a fir-tree on a hill,
    An old slave grinding at a heavy quern,
     A king sitting upon a chair of gold—
And all these things were wonderful and great;
But now I have grown nothing, knowing all.
Ah! Druid, Druid, how great webs of sorrow
Lay hidden in the small slate-coloured thing!

Who Goes With Fergus?

WHO will go drive with Fergus now,
And pierce the deep wood's woven shade,
And dance upon the level shore?
Young man, lift up your russet brow,
And lift your tender eyelids, maid,
And brood on hopes and fear no more.

And no more turn aside and brood
Upon love's bitter mystery;
For Fergus rules the brazen cars,
And rules the shadows of the wood,
And the white breast of the dim sea
And all dishevelled wandering stars.

The Two Trees

BELOVED, gaze in thine own heart,
The holy tree is growing there;
From joy the holy branches start,
And all the trembling flowers they bear.
The changing colour of its fruit
Have dowered the stars with merry light;
The surety of its hidden root
Has planted quiet in the night;
The shaking of its leafy head
Has given the waves their melody,
And made my lips and music wed,
Murmuring a wizard song for thee.
There the Loves a circle go,
The flaming circle of our days,
Gyring, spiring to and fro
In those great ignorant leafy ways;
Remembering all that shaken hair
And how the wingèd sandals dart,
Thine eyes grow full of tender care:
Beloved, gaze in thine own heart.

Gaze no more in the bitter glass
The demons, with their subtle guile,
Lift up before us when they pass,
Or only gaze a little while;
For there a fatal image grows
That the stormy night receives,
Roots half hidden under snows,
Broken boughs and blackened leaves.
For all things turn to barrenness
In the dim glass the demons hold,

The glass of outer weariness,
Made when God slept in times of old.
There, through the broken branches, go
The ravens of unresting thought;
Flying, crying, to and fro,
Cruel claw and hungry throat,
Or else they stand and sniff the wind,
And shake their ragged wings; alas!
Thy tender eyes grow all unkind:
Gaze no more in the bitter glass.

The White Birds

I WOULD that we were, my beloved, white birds on the
foam of the sea!
We tire of the flame of the meteor, before it can fade
and flee;
And the flame of the blue star of twilight, hung low
on the rim of the sky,
Has awaked in our hearts, my beloved, a sadness that
may not die.

A weariness comes from those dreamers, dew-dabbled,
the lily and rose;
Ah, dream not of them, my beloved, the flame of the
meteor that goes,
Or the flame of the blue star that lingers hung low in
the fall of the dew:
For I would we were changed to white birds on the
wandering foam: I and you!

I am haunted by numberless islands, and many a
Danaan shore,
Where Time would surely forget us, and Sorrow come
near us no more;
Soon far from the rose and the lily and fret of the
flames would we be,
Were we only white birds, my beloved, buoyed out on
the foam of the sea!

The Countess Cathleen in Paradise

ALL the heavy days are over;
Leave the body's coloured pride
Underneath the grass and clover,
With the feet laid side by side.

Bathed in flaming founts of duty
She'll not ask a haughty dress;
Carry all that mournful beauty
To the scented oaken press.

Did the kiss of Mother Mary
Put that music in her face?
Yet she goes with footstep wary,
Full of earth's old timid grace.

'Mong the feet of angels seven
What a dancer glimmering!
All the heavens bow down to Heaven,
Flame to flame and wing to wing.

When You Are Old

When you are old and grey and full of sleep,
And nodding by the fire, take down this book,
And slowly read, and dream of the soft look
Your eyes had once, and of their shadows deep;

How many loved your moments of glad grace,
And loved your beauty with love false or true,
But one man loved the pilgrim soul in you,
And loved the sorrows of your changing face;

And bending down beside the glowing bars,
Murmur, a little sadly, how Love fled
And paced upon the mountains overhead
And hid his face amid a crowd of stars.

The Cap and Bells

THE jester walked in the garden:
The garden had fallen still;
He bade his soul rise upward
And stand on her window-sill.

It rose in a straight blue garment,
When owls began to call:
It had grown wise-tongued by thinking
Of a quiet and light footfall;

But the young queen would not listen;
She rose in her pale night-gown;
She drew in the heavy casement
And pushed the latches down.

He bade his heart go to her,
When the owls called out no more;
In a red and quivering garment
It sang to her through the door.

It had grown sweet-tongued by dreaming
Of a flutter of flower-like hair;
But she took up her fan from the table
And waved it off on the air.

'I have cap and bells,' he pondered,
'I will send them to her and die';
And when the morning whitened
He left them where she went by.

She laid them upon her bosom,
Under a cloud of her hair,
And her red lips sang them a love-song
Till stars grew out of the air.

She opened her door and her window,
And the heart and the soul came through,
To her right hand came the red one,
To her left hand came the blue.

They set up a noise like crickets,
A chattering wise and sweet,
And her hair was a folded flower
And the quiet of love in her feet.

He Wishes for the Cloths of Heaven

HAD I the heavens' embroidered cloths,
Enwrought with golden and silver light,
The blue and the dim and the dark cloths
Of night and light and the half-light,
I would spread the cloths under your feet:
But I, being poor, have only my dreams;
I have spread my dreams under your feet;
Tread softly because you tread on my dreams.

The Lover Tells of the Rose in his Heart

ALL things uncomely and broken, all things worn
out and old,
The cry of a child by the roadway, the creak of a
lumbering cart,
The heavy steps of the ploughman, splashing the
wintry mould,
Are wronging your image that blossoms a rose in the
deeps of my heart.

The wrong of unshapely things is a wrong too
great to be told;
I hunger to build them anew and sit on a
green knoll apart,
With the earth and the sky and the water, re-made, like a
casket of gold
For my dreams of your image that blossoms a rose in the
deeps of my heart.

The Fiddler of Dooney

WHEN I play on my fiddle in Dooney,
Folk dance like a wave of the sea;
My cousin is priest in Kilvarnet,
My brother in Mocharabuiee.

I passed my brother and cousin:
They read in their books of prayer;
I read in my book of songs
I bought at the Sligo fair.

When we come at the end of time
To Peter sitting in state,
He will smile on the three old spirits,
But call me first through the gate;

For the good are always the merry,
Save by an evil chance,
And the merry love the fiddle,
And the merry love to dance:

And when the folk there spy me,
They will all come up to me,
With 'Here is the fiddler of Dooney!'
And dance like a wave of the sea.

The Song of Wandering Aengus

I WENT out to the hazel wood,
Because a fire was in my head,
And cut and peeled a hazel wand,
And hooked a berry to a thread;
And when white moths were on the wing,
And moth-like stars were flickering out,
I dropped the berry in a stream
And caught a little silver trout.

When I had laid it on the floor
I went to blow the fire aflame,
But something rustled on the floor,
And some one called me by my name:
It had become a glimmering girl
With apple blossom in her hair
Who called me by my name and ran
And faded through the brightening air.

Though I am old with wandering
Through hollow lands and hilly lands,
I will find out where she has gone,
And kiss her lips and take her hands;
And walk among long dappled grass,
And pluck till time and times are done
The silver apples of the moon,
The golden apples of the sun.

Never Give All the Heart

NEVER give all the heart, for love
Will hardly seem worth thinking of
To passionate women if it seem
Certain, and they never dream
That it fades out from kiss to kiss;
For everything that's lovely is
But a brief, dreamy, kind delight.
O never give the heart outright,
For they, for all smooth lips can say,
Have given their hearts up to play.
And who could play it well enough
If deaf and dumb and blind with love?
He that made this knows all the cost,
For he gave all his heart and lost.

The Ragged Wood

O HURRY where by water among the trees
The delicate-stepping stage and his lady sigh,
When they have but looked upon their images –
Would none had ever loved but you and I!

Or have you heard that sliding silver-shoed
Pale silver-proud queen-woman of the sky,
When the sun looked out of his golden hood? –
O that none ever loved but you and I!

O hurry to the ragged wood, for there
I will drive all those lovers out and cry –
O my share of the world, O yellow hair!
No one has ever loved but you and I.

O Do Not Love Too Long

SWEETHEART, do not love too long:
I loved long and long,
And grew to be out of fashion
Like an old song.

All through the years of our youth
Neither could have known
Their own thought from the other's,
We were so much at one.

But O, in a minute she changed –
O do not love too long,
Or you will grow out of fashion
Like an old song.

At Galway Races

THERE where the course is,
Delight makes all of the one mind,
The riders upon the galloping horses,
The crowd that closes in behind:
We, too, had good attendance once,
Hearers and hearteners of the work;
Aye, horsemen for companions,
Before the merchant and the clerk
Breathed on the world with timid breath.
Sing on: somewhere at some new moon,
We'll learn that sleeping is not death,
Hearing the whole earth change its tune,
Its flesh being wild, and it again
Crying aloud as the racecourse is,
And we find hearteners among men
That ride upon horses.

No Second Troy

WHY should I blame her that she filled my days
With misery, or that she would of late
Have taught to ignorant men most violent ways,
Or hurled the little streets upon the great,
Had they but courage equal to desire?
What could have made her peaceful with a mind
That nobleness made simple as a fire,
With beauty like a tightened bow, a kind
That is not natural in an age like this,
Being high and solitary and most stern?
Why, what could she have done, being what she is?
Was there another Troy for her to burn?

Words

I HAD this thought a while ago,
'My darling cannot understand
What I have done, or what would do
In this blind bitter land.'

And I grew weary of the sun
Until my thoughts cleared up again,
Remembering that the best I have done
Was done to make it plain;

That every year I have cried, 'At length
My darling understands it all,
Because I have come into my strength,
And words obey my call';

That had she done so who can say
What would have shaken from the sieve?
I might have thrown poor words away
And been content to live.

A Woman Homer Sung

IF any man drew near
When I was young,
I thought, 'He holds her dear,'
And shook with hate and fear.
But O! 'twas bitter wrong
If he could pass her by
With an indifferent eye.

Whereon I wrote and wrought,
And now, being grey,
I dream that I have brought
To such a pitch my thought
That coming time can say,
'He shadowed in a glass
What thing her body was.'

For she had fiery blood
When I was young,
And trod so sweetly proud
As 'twere upon a cloud,
A woman Homer sung,
That life and letters seem
But an heroic dream.

I To a Child Dancing in the Wind

DANCE there upon the shore;
What need have you to care
For wind or water's roar?
And tumble out your hair
That the salt drops have wet;
Being young you have not known
The fool's triumph, nor yet
Love lost as soon as won,
Nor the best labourer dead
And all the sheaves to bind.
What need have you to dread
The monstrous crying of wind?

II Two Years Later

HAS no one said those daring
Kind eyes should be more learn'd?
Or warned you how despairing
The moths are when they are burned?
I could have warned you; but you are young,
So we speak a different tongue.

O you will take whatever's offered
And dream that all the world's a friend,
Suffer as your mother suffered,
Be as broken in the end.
But I am old and you are young,
And I speak a barbarous tongue.

The Cold Heaven

SUDDENLY I saw the cold and rook-delighting heaven
That seemed as though ice burned and was but the more ice,
And thereupon imagination and heart were driven
So wild that every casual thought of that and this
Vanished, and left but memories, that should be out of season
With the hot blood of youth, of love crossed long ago;
And I took all the blame out of all sense and reason,
Until I cried and trembled and rocked to and fro,
Riddled with light. Ah! when the ghost begins to quicken,
Confusion of the death-bed over, is it sent
Out naked on the roads, as the books say, and stricken
By the injustice of the skies for punishment?

The Magi

NOW as at all times I can see in the mind's eye,
In their stiff, painted clothes, the pale unsatisfied ones
Appear and disappear in the blue depth of the sky
With all their ancient faces like rain-beaten stones,
And all their helms of silver hovering side by side,
And all their eyes still fixed, hoping to find once more,
Being by Calvary's turbulence unsatisfied,
The uncontrollable mystery on the bestial floor.

The Mountain Tomb

POUR wine and dance if manhood still have pride,
Bring roses if the rose be yet in bloom;
The cataract smokes upon the mountain side,
Our Father Rosicross is in his tomb.

Pull down the blinds, bring fiddle and clarionet
That there be no foot silent in the room
Nor mouth from kissing, nor from wine unwet;
Our Father Rosicross is in his tomb.

In vain, in vain; the cataract still cries;
The everlasting taper lights the gloom;
All wisdom shut into his onyx eyes,
Our Father Rosicross sleeps in his tomb.

On Those That Hated 'The Playboy of the Western World', 1907

ONCE, when midnight smote the air,
Eunuchs ran through Hell and met
On every crowded street to stare
Upon great Juan riding by:
Even like these to rail and sweat
Staring upon his sinewy thigh.

September 1913

WHAT need you, being come to sense,
But fumble in a greasy till
And add the halfpence to the pence
And prayer to shivering prayer, until
You have dried the marrow from the bone?
For men were born to pray and save:
Romantic Ireland's dead and gone,
It's with O'Leary in the grave.

Yet they were of a different kind,
The names that stilled your childish play,
They have gone about the world like wind,
But little time had they to pray
For whom the hangman's rope was spun,
And what, God help us, could they save?
Romantic Ireland's dead and gone,
It's with O'Leary in the grave.

Was it for this the wild geese spread
The grey wing upon every tide;
For this that all that blood was shed,
For this Edward Fitzgerald died,
And Robert Emmet and Wolfe Tone,
All that delirium of the brave?
Romantic Ireland's dead and gone,
It's with O'Leary in the grave.

Yet could we turn the years again,
And call those exiles as they were
In all their loneliness and pain,
You'd cry, 'Some woman's yellow hair
Has maddened every mother's son':
But let them be, they're dead and gone,
They're with O'Leary in the grave.

A Coat

I MADE my song a coat
Covered with embroideries
Out of old mythologies
From heel to throat;
But the fools caught it,
Wore it in the world's eyes
As though they'd wrought it.
Song, let them take it,
For there's more enterprise
In walking naked.

The Wild Swans at Coole

THE trees are in their autumn beauty,
The woodland paths are dry,
Under the October twilight the water
Mirrors a still sky;
Upon the brimming water among the stones
Are nine-and-fifty swans.

The nineteenth autumn has come upon me
Since I first made my count;
I saw, before I had well finished,
All suddenly mount
And scatter wheeling in great broken rings
Upon their clamorous wings.

I have looked upon those brilliant creatures,
And now my heart is sore.
All's changed since I, hearing at twilight,
The first time on this shore,
The bell-beat of their wings above my head,
Trod with a lighter tread.

Unwearied still, lover by lover,
They paddle in the cold
Companionable streams or climb the air;
Their hearts have not grown old;
Passion or conquest, wander where they will,
Attend upon them still.

But now they drift on the still water,
Mysterious, beautiful;
Among what rushes will they build,
By what lake's edge or pool
Delight men's eyes when I awake some day
To find they have flown away?

An Irish Airman Foresees His Death

I KNOW that I shall meet my fate
Somewhere among the clouds above;
Those that I fight I do not hate,
Those that I guard I do not love;
My country is Kiltartan Cross,
My countrymen Kiltartan's poor,
No likely end could bring them loss
Or leave them happier than before.
Nor law, nor duty bade me fight,
Nor public men, nor cheering crowds,
A lonely impulse of delight
Drove to this tumult in the clouds;
I balanced all, brought all to mind,
The years to come seemed waste of breath,
A waste of breath the years behind
In balance with this life, this death.

The Dawn

I WOULD be ignorant as the dawn
That has looked down
On that old queen measuring a town
With the pin of a brooch,
Or on the withered men that saw
From their pedantic Babylon
The careless planets in their courses,
The stars fade out where the moon comes,
And took their tablets and did sums;
I would be ignorant as the dawn
That merely stood, rocking the glittering coach
Above the cloudy shoulders of the horses;
I would be – for no knowledge is worth a straw –
Ignorant and wanton as the dawn.

Broken Dreams

THERE is grey in your hair.
Young men no longer suddenly catch their breath
When you are passing;
But maybe some old gaffer mutters a blessing
Because it was your prayer
Recovered him upon the bed of death.
For your sole sake – that all heart's ache have known,
And given to others all heart's ache,
From meagre girlhood's putting on
Burdensome beauty for your sole sake
Heaven has put away the stroke of her doom,
So great her portion in that peace you make
By merely walking in a room.

Your beauty can but leave among us
Vague memories, nothing but memories.
A young man when the old men are done talking
Will say to an old man, 'Tell me of that lady
The poet stubborn with his passion sang us
When age might well have chilled his blood.'

Vague memories, nothing but memories,
But in the grave all, all, shall be renewed.
The certainty that I shall see that lady
Leaning or standing or walking
In the first loveliness of womanhood,
And with the fervour of my youthful eyes,
Has set me muttering like a fool.

You are more beautiful than any one,
And yet your body had a flaw:
Your small hands were not beautiful,
And I am afraid that you will run
And paddle to the wrist
In that mysterious, always brimming lake
Where those that have obeyed the holy law
Paddle and are perfect. Leave unchanged
The hands that I have kissed,
For old sake's sake.

The last stroke of midnight dies.
All day in the one chair
From dream to dream and rhyme to rhyme I have ranged
In rambling talk with an image of air:
Vague memories, nothing but memories.

Easter 1916

I HAVE met them at close of day
Coming with vivid faces
From counter or desk among grey
Eighteenth-century houses.
I have passed with a nod of the head
Or polite meaningless words,
Or have lingered awhile and said
Polite meaningless words,
And thought before I had done
Of a mocking tale or a gibe
To please a companion
Around the fire at the club,
Being certain that they and I
But lived where motley is worn:
All changed, changed utterly:
A terrible beauty is born.

That woman's days were spent
In ignorant good-will
Her nights in argument
Until her voice grew shrill.
What voice more sweet than hers
When, young and beautiful,
She rode to harriers?
This man had kept a school
And rode our wingèd horse;
This other his helper and friend
Was coming into his force;
He might have won fame in the end,

So sensitive his nature seemed,
So daring and sweet his thought.
This other man I had dreamed
A drunken, vainglorious lout.
He had done most bitter wrong
To some who are near my heart,
Yet I number him in the song;
He, too, has resigned his part
In the casual comedy;
He, too, has been changed in his turn,
Transformed utterly:
A terrible beauty is born.

Hearts with one purpose alone
Through summer and winter seem
Enchanted to stone
To trouble the living stream.
The horse that comes from the road,
The rider, the birds that range
From cloud to tumbling cloud,
Minute by minute they change;
A shadow of cloud on the stream
Changes minute by minute;
A horse-hoof slides on the brim,
And a horse splashes within it;
The long-legged moor-hens dive,
And hens to moor-cocks call;
Minute by minute they live:
The stone's in the midst of all.

Too long a sacrifice
Can make a stone of the heart.
O when may it suffice?
That is Heaven's part, our part

To murmur name upon name,
As a mother names her child
When sleep at last has come
On limbs that had run wild.
What is it but nightfall?
No, no, not night but death;
Was it needless death after all?
For England may keep faith
For all that is done and said.
We know their dream; enough
To know they dreamed and are dead;
And what if excess of love
Bewildered them till they died?
I write it out in a verse –
MacDonagh and MacBride
And Connolly and Pearse
Now and in time to be,
Wherever green is worn,
Are changed, changed utterly:
A terrible beauty is born.

Under Saturn

DO not because this day I have grown saturnine
Imagine that lost love, inseparable from my thought
Because I have no other youth, can make me pine;
For how should I forget the wisdom that you brought,
The comfort that you made? Although my wits have gone
On a fantastic ride, my horse's flanks are spurred
By childish memories of an old cross Pollexfen,
And of a Middleton, whose name you never heard,
And of a red-haired Yeats whose looks, although he died
Before my time, seem like a vivid memory.
You heard that labouring man who had served my people.
He said
Upon the open road, near to the Sligo quay –
No, no, not said, but cried it out – 'You have come again,
And surely after twenty years it was time to come.'
I am thinking of a child's vow sworn in vain
Never to leave that valley his fathers called their home.

November 1919

A Prayer for My Daughter

ONCE more the storm is howling, and half hid
Under this cradle-hood and coverlid
My child sleeps on. There is no obstacle
But Gregory's wood and one bare hill
Whereby the haystack- and roof-levelling wind,
Bred on the Atlantic, can be stayed;
And for an hour I have walked and prayed
Because of the great gloom that is in my mind.

I have walked and prayed for this young child an hour
And heard the sea-wind scream upon the tower,
And under the arches of the bridge, and scream
In the elms above the flooded stream;
Imagining in excited reverie
That the future years had come,
Dancing to a frenzied drum,
Out of the murderous innocence of the sea.

May she be granted beauty and yet not
Beauty to make a stranger's eye distraught,
Or hers before a looking-glass, for such,
Being made beautiful overmuch,
Consider beauty a sufficient end,
Lose natural kindness and maybe
The heart-revealing intimacy
That chooses right, and never find a friend.

Helen being chosen found life flat and dull
And later had much trouble from a fool,
While that great Queen, that rose out of the spray,
Being fatherless could have her way
Yet chose a bandy-leggèd smith for man.
It's certain that fine women eat
A crazy salad with their meat
Whereby the Horn of Plenty is undone.

In courtesy I'd have her chiefly learned;
Hearts are not had as a gift but hearts are earned
By those that are not entirely beautiful;
Yet many, that have played the fool
For beauty's very self, has charm made wise,
And many a poor man that has roved,
Loved and thought himself beloved,
From a glad kindness cannot take his eyes.

May she become a flourishing hidden tree
That all her thoughts may like the linnet be,
And have no business but dispensing round
Their magnanimities of sound,
Nor but in merriment begin a chase,
Nor but in merriment a quarrel.
O may she live like some green laurel
Rooted in one dear perpetual place.

My mind, because the minds that I have loved,
The sort of beauty that I have approved,
Prosper but little, has dried up of late,
Yet knows that to be choked with hate
May well be of all evil chances chief.
If there's no hatred in a mind
Assault and battery of the wind
Can never tear the linnet from the leaf.

An intellectual hatred is the worst,
So let her think opinions are accursed.
Have I not seen the loveliest woman born
Out of the mouth of Plenty's horn,
Because of her opinionated mind
Barter that horn and every good
By quiet natures understood
For an old bellows full of angry wind?

Considering that, all hatred driven hence,
The soul recovers radical innocence
And learns at last that it is self-delighting,
Self-appeasing, self-affrighting,
And that its own sweet will is Heaven's will;
She can, though every face should scowl
And every windy quarter howl
Or every bellows burst, be happy still.

And may her bridegroom bring her to a house
Where all's accustomed, ceremonious;
For arrogance and hatred are the wares
Peddled in the thoroughfares.
How but in custom and in ceremony
Are innocence and beauty born?
Ceremony's a name for the rich horn,
And custom for the spreading laurel tree.

Sailing to Byzantium

I

THAT is no country for old men. The young
In one another's arms, birds in the trees
– Those dying generations – at their song,
The salmon-falls, the mackerel-crowded seas,
Fish, flesh, or fowl, commend all summer long
Whatever is begotten, born, and dies.
Caught in that sensual music all neglect
Monuments of unageing intellect.

II

An aged man is but a paltry thing,
A tattered coat upon a stick, unless
Soul clap its hands and sing, and louder sing
For every tatter in its mortal dress,
Nor is there singing school but studying
Monuments of its own magnificence;
And therefore I have sailed the seas and come
To the holy city of Byzantium.

III

O sages standing in God's holy fire
As in the gold mosaic of a wall,
Come from the holy fire, perne in a gyre,
And be the singing-masters of my soul
Consume my heart away; sick with desire
And fastened to a dying animal
It knows not what it is; and gather me
Into the artifice of eternity.

IV

Once out of nature I shall never take
My bodily form from any natural thing,
But such a form as Grecian goldsmiths make
Of hammered gold and gold enamelling
To keep a drowsy Emperor awake;
Or set upon a golden bough to sing
To lords and ladies of Byzantium
Of what is past, or passing, or to come.

Leda and the Swan

A SUDDEN blow: the great wings beating still
Above the staggering girl, her thighs caressed
By the dark webs, her nape caught in his bill,
He holds her helpless breast upon his breast.

How can those terrified vague fingers push
The feathered glory from her loosening thighs?
And how can body, laid in that white rush,
But feel the strange heart beating where it lies?

A shudder in the loins engenders there
The broken wall, the burning roof and tower
And Agamemnon dead.
Being so caught up,
So mastered by the brute blood of the air,
Did she put on his knowledge with his power
Before the indifferent beak could let her drop?

A Man Young and Old

EXTRACT

I First Love

THOUGH nurtured like the sailing moon
In beauty's murderous brood,
She walked awhile and blushed awhile
And on my pathway stood
Until I thought her body bore
A heart of flesh and blood.

But since I laid a hand thereon
And found a heart of stone
I have attempted many things
And not a thing is done,
For every hand is lunatic
That travels on the moon.

She smiled and that transfigured me
And left me but a lout,
Maundering here, and maundering there,
Emptier of thought
Than the heavenly circuit of its stars
When the moon sails out.

III The Mermaid

A mermaid found a swimming lad,
Picked him for her own,
Pressed her body to his body,
Laughed; and plunging down
Forgot in cruel happiness
That even lovers drown.

V *The Empty Cup*

A crazy man that found a cup,
When all but dead of thirst,
Hardly dared to wet his mouth
Imagining, moon-accursed,
That another mouthful
And his beating heart would burst.
October last I found it too
But found it dry as bone,
And for that reason am I crazed
And my sleep is gone.

VI *His Memories*

We should be hidden from their eyes,
Being but holy shows
And bodies broken like a thorn
Whereon the bleak north blows,
To think of buried Hector
And that none living knows.

The women take so little stock
In what I do or say
They'd sooner leave their cosseting
To hear a jackass bray;
My arms are like the twisted thorn
And yet there beauty lay;

The first of all the tribe lay there
And did such pleasure take –
She who had brought great Hector down
And put all Troy to wreck –
That she cried into this ear,
'Strike me if I shriek.'

VII *The Friends of his Youth*

Laughter not time destroyed my voice
And put that crack in it,
And when the moon's pot-bellied
I get a laughing fit,
For that old Madge comes down the lane,
A stone upon her breast,
And a cloak wrapped about the stone,
And she can get no rest
With singing hush and hush-a-bye;
She that has been wild
And barren as a breaking wave
Thinks that the stone's a child.
And Peter that had great affairs
And was a pushing man
Shrieks, 'I am King of the Peacocks,'
And perches on a stone;
And then I laugh till tears run down
And the heart thumps at my side,
Remembering that her shriek was love
And that he shrieks from pride.

VIII *Summer and Spring*

We sat under an old thorn-tree
And talked away the night,
Told all that had been said or done
Since first we saw the light,
And when we talked of growing up
Knew that we'd halved a soul
And fell the one in t'other's arms
That we might make it whole;
Then Peter had a murdering look,
For it seemed that he and she
Had spoken of their childish days
Under that very tree.
O what a bursting out there was,
And what a blossoming,
When we had all the summer-time
And she had all the spring!

Wisdom

THE true faith discovered was
When painted panel, statuary,
Glass-mosaic, window-glass,
Amended what was told awry
By some peasant gospeller;
Swept the sawdust from the floor
Of that working-carpenter.
Miracle had its playtime where
In damask clothed and on a seat
Chryselephantine, cedar-boarded,
His majestic Mother sat
Stitching at a purple hoarded
That He might be nobly breeched
In starry towers of Babylon
Noah's freshet never reached.
King Abundance got Him on
Innocence; and Wisom He.
That cognomen sounded best
Considering what wild infancy
Drove horror from His Mother's breast.

sit, the heart's a wonder; and, I'm thinking, there

A Dialogue of Self and Soul

I

My Soul. I summon to the winding ancient stair;
Set all your mind upon the steep ascent,
Upon the broken, crumbling battlement,
Upon the breathless starlit air,
Upon the star that marks the hidden pole;
Fix every wandering thought upon
That quarter where all thought is done:
Who can distinguish darkness from the soul?

My Self. The consecrated blade upon my knees
Is Sato's ancient blade, still as it was,
Still razor-keen, still like a looking-glass
Unspotted by the centuries;
That flowering, silken, old embroidery, torn
From some court-lady's dress and round
The wooden scabbard bound and wound,
Can, tattered, still protect, faded adorn.

My Soul. Why should the imagination of a man
Long past his prime remember things that are
Emblematical of love and war?
Think of ancestral night that can,
If but imagination scorn the earth
And intellect its wandering
To this and that and t'other thing,
Deliver from the crime of death and birth.

My Self. Montashigi, third of his family, fashioned it
Five hundred years ago, about it lie
Flowers from I know not what embroidery –
Heart's purple – and all these I set

For emblems of the day against the tower
Emblematical of the night,
And claim as by a soldier's right
A charter to commit the crime once more.

My Soul. Such fullness in that quarter overflows
And falls into the basin of the mind
That man is stricken deaf and dumb and blind,
For intellect no longer knows
Is from the *Ought,* or *Knower* from the *Known* —
That is to say, ascends to Heaven;
Only the dead can be forgiven;
But when I think of that my tongue's a stone.

II

My Self. A living man is blind and drinks his drop.
What matter if the ditches are impure?
What matter if I live it all once more?
Endure that toil of growing up;
The ignominy of boyhood; the distress
Of boyhood changing into man;
The unfinished man and his pain
Brought face to face with his own clumsiness;

The finished man among his enemies? —
How in the name of Heaven can he escape
That defiling and disfigured shape
The mirror of malicious eyes
Casts upon his eyes until at last
He thinks that shape must be his shape?
And what's the good of an escape
If honour find him in the wintry blast?

And yet again, if it be life to pitch
Into the frog-spawn of a blind man's ditch
A blind man battering blind men;
Or into that most fecund ditch of all,
The folly that man does
Or must suffer, if he woos
A proud woman not kindred of his soul.

I am content to follow to its source
Every event in action or in thought;
Measure the lot; forgive myself the lot!
When such as I cast out remorse
So great a sweetness flows into the breast
We must laugh and we must sing,
We are blest by everything.
Everything we look upon is blest.

Death

NOR dread nor hope attend
A dying animal;
A man awaits his end
Dreading and hoping all;
Many times he died,
Many times rose again.
A great man in his pride
Confronting murderous men
Casts derision upon
Supersession of breath;
He knows death to the bone –
Man has created death.

Coole Park, 1929

I MEDITATE upon a swallow's flight,
Upon an aged woman and her house,
A sycamore and lime-tree lost in night
Although that western cloud is luminous,
Great works constructed there in nature's spite
For scholars and for poets after us,
Thoughts long knitted into a single thought,
A dance-like glory that those walls begot.

There Hyde before he had beaten into prose
That noble blade the Muses buckled on,
There one that ruffled in a manly pose
For all his timid heart, there that slow man,
That meditative man, John Synge, and those
Impetuous men, Shawe-Taylor and Hugh Lane,
Found pride established in humility,
A scene well set and excellent company.

They came like swallows and like swallows went,
And yet a woman's powerful character
Could keep a swallow to its first intent;
And half a dozen in formation there,
That seemed to whirl upon a compass-point,
Found certainty upon the dreaming air,
The intellectual sweetness of those lines
That cut through time or cross it withershins.
Here, traveller, scholar, poet, take your stand
When all those rooms and passages are gone,

When nettles wave upon a shapeless mound
And saplings root among the broken stone,
And dedicate – eyes bent upon the ground,
Back turned upon the brightness of the sun
And all the sensuality of the shade –
A moment's memory to that laurelled head.

The Crazed Moon

CRAZED through much child-bearing
The moon is staggering in the sky;
Moon-struck by the despairing
Glances of her wandering eye
We grope, and grope in vain,
For children born of her pain.

Children dazed or dead!
When she in all her virginal pride
First trod on the mountain's head
What stir ran through the countryside
Where every foot obeyed her glance!
What manhood led the dance!

Fly-catchers of the moon,
Our hands are blenched, our fingers seem
But slender needles of bone;
Blenched by that malicious dream
They are spread wide that each
May rend what comes in reach.

The Circus Animals' Desertion

I

I SOUGHT a theme and sought for it in vain,
I sought it daily for six weeks or so.
Maybe at last, being but a broken man,
I must be satisfied with my heart, although
Winter and summer till old age began
My circus animals were all on show,
Those stilted boys, that burnished chariot,
Lion and woman and the Lord knows what.

II

What can I but enumerate old themes?
First that sea-rider Oisin led by the nose
Through three enchanted island, allegorical dreams,
Vain gaiety, vain battle, vain repose,
Themes of the embittered heart, or so it seems,
That might adorn old songs or courtly shows;
But what cared I that set him on to ride,
I, starved for the bosom of his faery bride?

And then a counter-truth filled out its play,
The Countess Cathleen was the name I gave it;
She, pity-crazed, had given her soul away,
But masterful Heaven had intervened to save it.
I thought my dear must her own soul destroy,
So did fanaticism and hate enslave it,
And this brought forth a dream and soon enough
This dream itself had all my thought and love.

And when the Fool and Blind Man stole the bread
Cuchulain fought the ungovernable sea;
Heart-mysteries there, and yet when all is said
It was the dream itself enchanted me:
Character isolated by a deed
To engross the present and dominate memory.
Players and painted stage took all my love,
And not those things that they were emblems of.

III

Those masterful images because complete
Grew in pure mind, but out of what began?
A mound of refuse or the sweepings of a street,
Old kettles, old bottles, and a broken can,
Old iron, old bones, old rags, that raving slut
Who keeps the till. Now that my ladder's gone,
I must lie down where all the ladders start,
In the foul rag-and-bone shop of the heart.

Come Gather Round Me, Parnellites

COME gather round me, Parnellites,
And praise our chosen man;
Stand upright on your legs awhile,
Stand upright while you can,
For soon we lie where he is laid,
And he is underground;
Come fill up all those glasses
And pass the bottle round.

And here's a cogent reason,
And I have many more,
He fought the might of England
And saved the Irish poor,
Whatever good a farmer's got
He brought it all to pass;
And here's another reason,
That Parnell loved a lass.

And here's a final reason,
He was of such a kind
Every man that sings a song
Keeps Parnell in his mind.
For Parnell was a proud man,
No prouder trod the ground,
And a proud man's a lovely man,
So pass the bottle round.

The bishops and the Party
That tragic story made,
A husband that had sold his wife
And after that betrayed;

But stories that live longest
Are sung above the glass,
And Parnell loved his country,
And Parnell loved his lass.

Why Should Not Old Men Be Mad

WHY should not old men be mad?
Some have known a likely lad
That had a sound fly-fisher's wrist
Turn to a drunken journalist;
A girl that knew all Dante once
Live to bear children to a dunce;
A Helen of social welfare dream,
Climb on a wagonette to scream.
Some think it a matter of course that chance
Should starve good men and bad advance,
That if their neighbours figured plain,
As though upon a lighted screen,
No single story would they find
Of an unbroken happy mind,
A finish worthy of the start.
Young men know nothing of this sort,
Observant old men know it well;
And when they know what old books tell,
And that no better can be had,
Know why an old man should be mad.

Index to First Lines

A crazy man that found a cup 76
All the heavy days are over...30
All things uncomely and broken, all things worn out
    and old 36
A mermaid found a swimming lad 75
A sudden blow: the great wings beating still 74

Beloved, gaze in thine own heart.....................................26

Come gather round me, Parnellites 91
Crazed through much child-bearing 87

Dance there upon the shore...50
Do not because this day I have grown saturnine 68
Down by the salley gardens 19

Had I the heavens' embroidered cloths 35

I had this thought a while ago..47
I have met them at close of day 65
I know that I shall meet my fate.......................................59
I made my song a coat..56
I meditate upon a swallow's flight 86
I sought a theme and sought for it in vain.......................88
I summon to the winding ancient stair 82
I went out to the hazel wood...40
I would be ignorant as the dawn 60
I would that we were, my beloved, white birds on the
    foam of the sea!...28
If any man drew near..48

Laughter not time destroyed my voice 78

Never give all the heart, for love 42
Nor dread nor hope attend 85
Now as at all times I can see in the mind's eye 51

O hurry where by water among the trees 44
Once more the storm is howling, and half hid 69
Once, when midnight smote the air 53

Pour wine and dance if manhood still have pride 52

Suddenly I saw the cold and rook-delighting heaven..........51
Sweetheart, do not love too long 44

That is no country for old men 73
The jester walked in the garden...33
The trees are in their autumn beauty 58
The true faith discovered was 80
There is grey in your hair 62
There where the course is 45
This whole day have I followed in the rocks 22
Though nurtured like the sailing moon...............................75

Your eyes that once were never weary
    of mine 14

We sat under an old thorn-tree 79
We should be hidden from their eyes 76
We who are old, old and gay 20
What need you, being come to sense 54
When I play on my fiddle in Dooney 38
When you are old and grey and full of sleep......................32
Where dips the rocky highland 16
Who will go drive with Fergus now 24
Why should I blame her that she filled my days 46
Why should not old men be mad 92

Notes for Illustrations

3   Detail from *Portrait of Yeats*, by Augustus John (Glasgow Art Gallery & Museum). Courtesy of The Bridgeman Art Library.

7   *Portrait of Yeats*, by Augustus John (Glasgow Art Gallery & Museum). Courtesy of The Bridgeman Art Library.

12   *W.B. Yeats*, 1907, sketch, by Augustus John (Tate Gallery, London). Courtesy of The Bridgeman Art Library.

15   *Ghirimeer, on the Upper Lake of Killarney*, by Unknown (Victoria & Albert Museum, London). Courtesy of The Bridgeman Art Library.

17   *Fairies in Flight*, by Arthur Rackham. Courtesy of The Charles Walker Collection at Images.

19   *The Briar Wood*, by Woodbine K. Hinchliff (Christopher Wood Gallery, London). Courtesy of The Bridgeman Art Library.

20-1   *Twilight Fantasies*, by Edward Robert Hughes (The Maas Gallery). Courtesy of The Bridgeman Art Library.

25   *A Woodland Glade*, by Paul Jacob Naftel (Christopher Wood Gallery, London). Courtesy of The Bridgeman Art Library.

27   Detail from *Woman at Dawn*, by Caspar-David Friedrich (Museum Folkwang, Essen, West Germany). Courtesy of The Bridgeman Art Library.

29   *The Storm*, by Nick Wells. Courtesy of The Foundry Creative Media Co. Ltd.

31   Design for *The Geneva Window*, showing Countess Cathleen by Yeats, by Harry Clarke (The Fine Art Society, London). Courtesy of The Bridgeman Art Library.

34   Chromolithograph, based on a manuscript miniature of the 15th Century. Courtesy of The Charles Walker Collection at Images.

37   *A Moment of Time* (panel), by Jack Butler Yeats (Phillips, London). Courtesy of The Bridgeman Art Library.

39   *The Blind Fiddler at Brathay*, by John Harden (Abbot Hall Art Gallery, Kendal). Courtesy of The Bridgeman Art Library.

41   *The Two Travellers*, by Jack Butler Yeats (Tate Gallery, London). Courtesy of The Bridgeman Art Library.

43   *The Sun May Shine and We Be Cold*, by Dante Gabriel Rossetti (Private Collection). Courtesy of The Bridgeman Art Library.

49   *The Evening Star*, by Sir Edward Burne-Jones (Private Collection). Courtesy of The Bridgeman Art Library.

52-3   *Irish Funeral*, by John Doyle (University of Dundee). Courtesy of The Bridgeman Art Library.

55   *Carrickfergus, Ireland*, by Thomas Creswick (Agnew & Sons, London). Courtesy of The Bridgeman Art Library.

57   *The Weaving of the Enchantress*, byThomas Matthews Rooke (Whitford & Hughes, London). Courtesy of The Bridgeman Art Library.

61   *Woman at Dawn*, by Caspar-David Friedrich. See page 27.

63   *In Memoriam*, by Evelyn de Morgan (The de Morgan Foundation, London). Courtesy of The Bridgeman Art Library.

71   *Our Daughter*, by Arthur Hughes (Christie's, London). Courtesy of The Bridgeman Art Library.

77   *Mermaid*, by Arthur Rackham. Courtesy of The Charles Walker Collection at Images.

81   Detail from *The Geneva Window*, by Harry Clark. See page 31.

84   *William Butler Yeats*, by Augustus John (Manchester City Art Galleries). Courtesy of The Bridgeman Art Library.

90   *Ballymahon, County Longford*, by Thomas Creswick (Agnew & Sons, London). Courtesy of The Bridgeman Art Library.

93   *The Pier*, by Jack Butler Yeats (Christie's, London). Courtesy of The Bridgeman Art Library.

96   Detail from *The Geneva Window*, by Harry Clark. See page 31.